A book for you from
Books for Nashville's Kids
Book'em
Nashville, Tennessee
www.bookem-kids.org

FROM J TO Z

THE SHAWN CARTER STORY

FROM J TO Z

THE SHAWN CARTER STORY

Megan Silianoff

Illustrated by Luke Harper

gatekeeper press

Published by Gatekeeper Press
3971 Hoover Rd. Suite 77
Columbus, OH 43123-2839

Illustrated by Luke Harper
Design by Merwin D. Loquias

ISBN (hardcover): 9781619849396

Printed in the United States of America

To Macy Carter Silianoff and Roman Wes Halpin.

May you each discover your passion in life and chase after it ferociously.

I'm not afraid of dyin'

I'm afraid of not tryin'

Every day, hit every wave,

like I'm Hawaiian

Jay Z

Once upon a time there was a place called The Marcy Projects.

There, in Brooklyn, lived generations who had few material objects.

One apartment housed lots of records

and a little boy named Shawn.

He lived with his mom, brother, and sisters

but his Daddy was gone.

Shawn loved poetry

and kept a notebook with hip hop rhymes.

He'd write about The Yankees, The Nets,

and his bags full of dimes.

When Shawn turned thirteen

he fell into the hustling industry.

It was an inevitable choice

that paid off fiscally.

In homage to his mentor, his friends called him Jazzy

and eventually just Jay Z.

Unbeknownst to everyone it was

a name destined for marquees.

As Shawn grew older so did the music vs. hustling discord inside his head.

His cousin urged him to give rap all he had and out the lyrics fled.

But no one would help Shawn make a record.

He needed a Prince Charming to his Cinderella.

So he decided to start his own record label

and named it Roc-A-Fella.

From there he made record after record and became a revolutionary artist.

He also was an entrepreneur and business mogul – he truly was the smartest.

One day destiny intervened

and Shawn met the Bonnie to his Clyde.

They were so crazy in love he put a ring on it

and she became his bride.

Shawn and Beyonce eventually had a baby,

as cute as she could be.

They raise her in the Empire State

and call her Blue Ivy.

The moral of Jay Z's story

couldn't be more crystal clear.

What land you come from doesn't matter,

it's how you persevere.

About the Author

This is Megan's third book following her memoir, *99 Problems But A Baby Ain't One - A Memoir about Cancer, Adoption, and My Love for Jay* (2013) and her e-book, *Everything I Know About Writing and Publishing A Book* (2015). Other creative pursuits include her popular lifestyle blog *Greetings from Texas*, and her creative services firm *Mad Meg Creative*. Megan resides in Houston, Texas with her daughter Macy Carter ("Carter" for Shawn Carter.) She has shared her own inspiring story and unique experiences at conferences and companies across the country including The US Air Force, Facebook, and Alt Summit. Her celebrity crushes include but are not limited to Jonah Hill, Bradley Cooper, and Chris Pratt. To learn more about Megan, follow her on instagram at @greetingsfromtx or visit her website www.megansilianoffwrites.com

About the Illustrator

Luke Harper is a student at UT Austin and has also taken classes at The Pratt Institute in New York City. To learn more about Luke's work follow him on instagram at @lukeharperdraws or visit his website www.lukeharperdraws.com

CPSIA information can be obtained
at www.ICGtesting.com
Printed in the USA
LVOW05*0539130416

483305LV00008B/14/P